Spellbound Science

BOOK 2

By
Brenda Keogh and Stuart Naylor
Illustrations Laura Murray

Acknowledgments

The following team of people have made this publication possible.
Our thanks are due to all of them for their creative ideas.

LAURA MURRAY
Illustrator
KATHRYN STAWPERT
Graphic Design

DAVID OSBORN
and
MELISSA WOOD
at Angel Solutions
software development

CHILDREN
at Smallwood CE Primary School,
Cheshire and TEACHERS there and
elsewhere, helping to develop the
stories and characters

BRIGID DOWNING, JANE MALONEY,
SHIRLEY SIMON and the
PUPPET PROJECT TEACHERS
exploring with us the potential of
puppets in science

JOHN DABELL
Narration
and
THE ROOFTOP GROUP
Sound engineering

KAY ROBERTS and FRANK ELLIS
at GlaxoSmithKline plc, their belief in our work will enable our puppet
characters, Jasmin and Benny, and their stories to engage children in
stimulating scientific experiences

And finally
JASMIN, BENNY, GRANDAD, MILLIE and LITTLE WIZARD,
whose ideas about science inspired us to create these stories.

Contents

Introduction

Welcome to Spellbound Science Book 2.

In this book you can read stories about Jasmin and Benny's science problems. Grandad, Millie and Little Wizard all try to help them.

NOTE

When you see this icon you **MUST** get an **ADULT'S** help.

4

A Trip to Planet Zorro

Ziggy and Zuggy went round every window in the spaceship one more time until all the windows were spotless. It was important to see where they were going when they took off and that it looked clean and tidy for when Jasmin and Benny arrived. Their holiday on Earth had lasted for nearly six weeks, and now it was time for them to return home to planet Zorro. Six weeks was a long enough holiday for anybody!

Jasmin and Benny were going with Ziggy and Zuggy to their planet. They were excited about going in the spaceship. "Brilliant!" said Jasmin. "Fantastic!" said Benny.

Ziggy and Zuggy were excited too. They were so excited that they kept switching on their anti-gravity devices and floating around.

Zuggy told Jasmin and Benny that they had packed four big boxes of ice cream, along with crisps, chocolate and plenty of fizzy drinks. It was going to be a very long trip, so they had bought lots of Jasmin and Benny's favourite food for the journey.

Benny looked worried. He really wanted to visit planet Zorro, but would his mum let him go if that was all there was to eat and drink? Jasmin looked pleased. She thought that ice cream, crisps, chocolate and fizzy drinks would be great. It should be everything that they needed.

Benny started to get upset. He was worried that he might be left behind. His mum always insisted that he had a healthy diet. He asked Ziggy and Zuggy if they were sure that ice cream, crisps, chocolate and fizzy drinks would be a healthy diet for humans on a long trip.

"Ggrrrrxyxylll," said Ziggy. "Mnmnyongggll," said Zuggy. They insisted that they had measured how much Earth people eat each day to make sure that Benny and Jasmin would have enough food to eat for the trip.

Then Benny had an idea. What if Ziggy and Zuggy were right? If there was plenty to eat and drink on the spaceship, perhaps his Mum wouldn't be concerned after all.

Just then Grandad and Millie arrived to see the spaceship. Jasmin and Benny were pleased to see them because they always had good ideas. Benny explained the problem to them. They all started to talk about the kind of food that Benny and Jasmin would need.

Try to think of your own ideas for finding out.
Here are some of our ideas for what you could do...

It would be fun to use computers and books to find out about different food groups, for example:

- ◎ proteins
- ◎ fats
- ◎ vitamins and minerals
- ◎ fruit and vegetables

- ◎ carbohydrates
- ◎ sugars

How about asking a chef, or a school cook, questions about healthy eating?

Are there people or organisations to write to for information?

All the information could go on a chart.

What if Jasmin and Benny couldn't take fresh meat or fresh vegetables on the journey?

Could they still have a balanced diet?

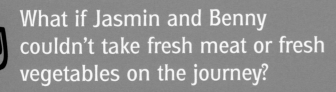
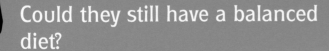

You could compare Ziggy and Zuggy's food with other people's ideas about what makes a balanced diet. Then you should be able to suggest what would be the best food for Benny and Jasmin to take.

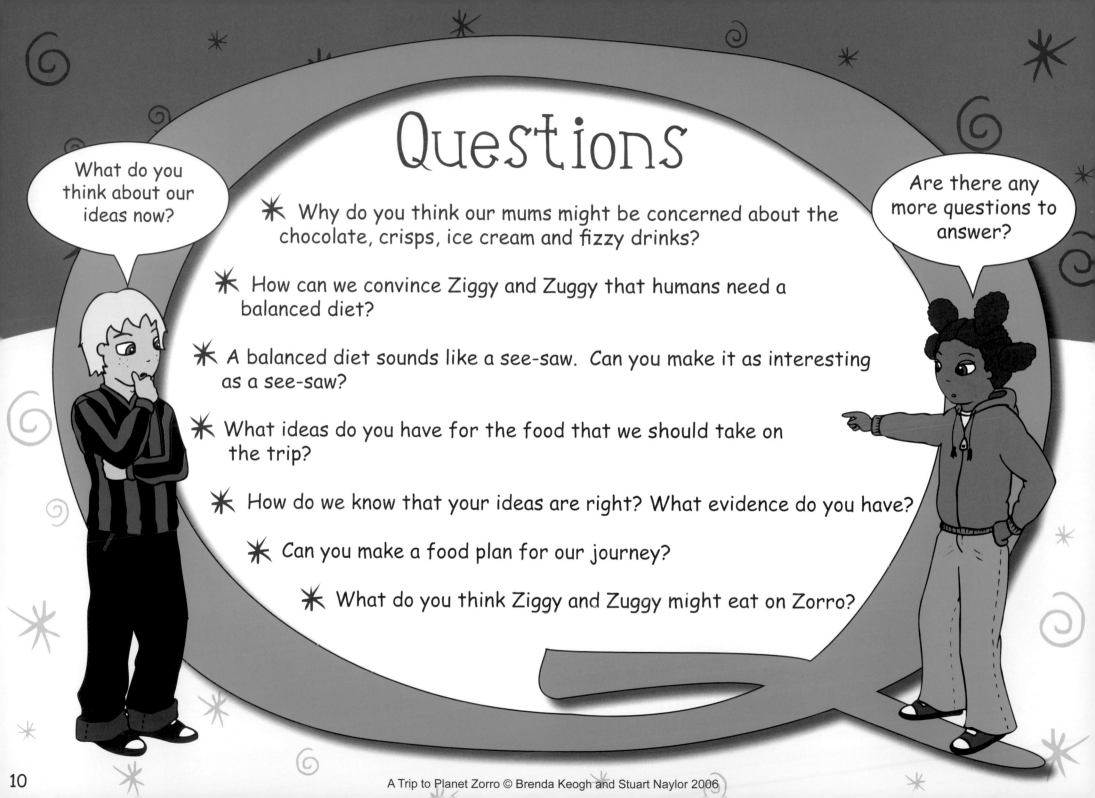

Questions

What do you think about our ideas now?

Are there any more questions to answer?

✳ Why do you think our mums might be concerned about the chocolate, crisps, ice cream and fizzy drinks?

✳ How can we convince Ziggy and Zuggy that humans need a balanced diet?

✳ A balanced diet sounds like a see-saw. Can you make it as interesting as a see-saw?

✳ What ideas do you have for the food that we should take on the trip?

✳ How do we know that your ideas are right? What evidence do you have?

✳ Can you make a food plan for our journey?

✳ What do you think Ziggy and Zuggy might eat on Zorro?

The big idea in this story is that humans need to have a balanced diet in order to keep healthy.

In order to keep healthy Benny and Jasmin will need water and a range of different types of foods. These include:

★ Fruit and vegetables

★ Bread, cereals and potatoes

★ Meat, fish or alternatives such as beans

★ Milk and dairy products

★ Some fats and sugars

They need different kinds of foods:

★ to give them energy to move around and to keep their bodies working well.

★ so that their bodies can grow.

★ to keep all the different parts of their bodies working properly.

★ so that their bodies can repair themselves and fight off disease.

The food and drink that Ziggy and Zuggy have bought contain a lot of sugar, salt and fat. If they eat these foods for a long time it will not keep them healthy. This means that they could put on weight, their hearts and blood circulation might be damaged and they might not grow properly.

The Ingobo Tree

Jasmin and Benny have just got back from their trip to planet Zorro. They have been given a special gift. It's a seed from the very rare Ingobo tree. It's the only Ingobo tree seed on Earth. They have just one seed. Now they want to grow the seed into a new tree.

Jasmin and Benny looked carefully at the seed and wondered how to make it grow. They'd bought the best compost they could afford from the garden centre. They had collected some plant pots and borrowed a trowel and a watering can. But what should they do next?

Jasmin suggested that they should leave the seed on the surface of the compost. That's where it would be in the forest when it starts to grow.

Benny wasn't sure. Wouldn't it get covered in leaves and twigs in the forest? Then it would be in the dark when it starts to grow. He thought that they should bury it in the compost.

Jasmin said "Put the pointed end upwards, Benny. The shoot comes from the pointed end, so it needs to go upwards." She handed the seed to Benny.

"I'm not sure, Jasmin" said Benny. "I think that the root comes from the pointed end so it should go downwards in the compost."

Jasmin said, "The seed will need water, but if it has too much water it might drown." She passed the watering can to Benny. Benny disagreed again. He said that it rains a lot in the forest so it will need lots of water. He filled the watering can so that it was overflowing.

Jasmin and Benny looked at each other. They were both feeling frustrated that they couldn't agree. Jasmin spoke first. "Look, Benny, we only have one seed so if we get it wrong that's it. We can't afford to make any mistakes." "Exactly!" Benny burst out. "If your ideas are wrong we will never get another chance."

Jasmin and Benny just stood there. They did want to get this right, but they didn't know the best way to grow the seed.

Just then Grandad and Millie arrived. They wanted to see the Ingobo tree seed. Benny explained the problem to them.

They all had different ideas. So they started to discuss what to do.

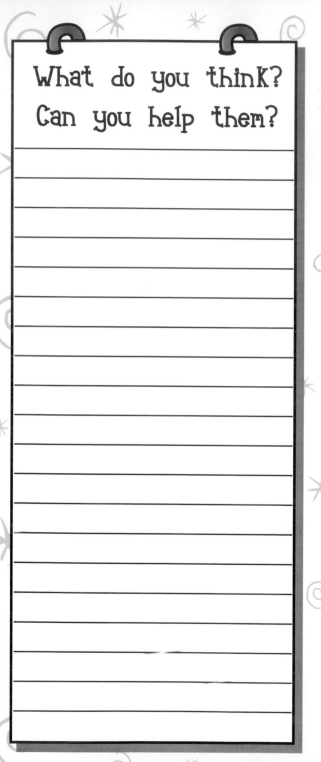

Try to think of your own ideas for finding out.
Here are some of our ideas for what you could do...

You could observe different kinds of seeds including ones from trees that have:

- ◎ dry seeds (e.g. sycamore or lime)
- ◎ nuts (e.g. hazel or beech)
- ◎ stones (e.g. plum or avocado)
- ◎ pips (e.g. apple or orange)

Some seeds are VERY POISONOUS!

Can you use your observations to make a simple key to sort and identify seeds?

Explore how seeds start to grow. Sow some seeds and watch what happens. Try sunflower seeds, peas, mustard or mung beans. Think of questions to answer as your seeds grow.

Why don't you investigate what makes a difference to how seeds start to grow?

For example:
- ◎ which way they are planted
- ◎ where they are planted
- ◎ how much light they have
- ◎ what they are planted in

What will you need to do to keep your test fair?

GROW A TREE!

Plant a seed such as an acorn and watch it grow over a year or more.

Questions

What do you think about our ideas now?

Are there any more questions to answer?

✳ Did you look at different seeds? What similarities and differences did you observe?

✳ What helped them to germinate?

✳ Were there any that didn't grow? Why do you think that was?

✳ What do you think would be the best way to grow the Ingobo seed?

✳ Why do you think some trees might become extinct? Is there anything we can do to stop it happening?

✳ How do we know your ideas are right? What evidence do you have?

✳ Can you create a seed box for the Ingobo tree seed? Put a picture on the front and planting instructions on the back.

The big idea in this story is that plants need special conditions to help them to germinate. As the plant grows bigger its needs will change.

Seeds need triggers to get them to start to grow (to germinate) at the right time.

★ For most seeds these triggers are water and warmth.

★ Some seeds may need a spell of cold weather.

★ Most seeds will start to grow without light. Food stored in the seed helps them to do this.

When the stored food is used up the plant needs to make more or it will die.

★ To produce food plants need sunlight.

★ Seedlings try to find the light. Without light they grow long and pale.

★ Plants turn green when light shines on them. The green part of the plant (known as chlorophyll) helps the plants to use sunlight and air to produce more food.

It doesn't matter which way up seeds are planted. The root will always grow downwards and the shoot will grow upwards to find the light.

Tree seeds often need special conditions to start to germinate.

Some tree seeds need to be very cold first or need a long soak in water.

Others just take a very long time.

18

Welcome to Earth

Jasmin and Benny were waiting at the interplanetary arrivals lounge. They had read their comics. They had bought a balloon. Now they were bored. They had seen the space ship arrive from planet Roxolon, and it was taking ages for Rebekah to come through Passport Control.

Benny spotted someone coming towards them. "This must be her," he whispered. Jasmin wasn't sure. She had only seen photographs of Rebekah. "You must be Jasmin and Benny," said Rebekah. She gave them both a special Roxolon greeting.

Benny handed Rebekah the balloon to welcome her to Earth. Her antennae glowed with pleasure. But before she could get hold of it, the balloon had floated away. "Why did it do that?" she asked in amazement. "Don't worry we can get you another one," said Jasmin. "Here, you can have my comic." Rebekah's antennae glowed again. "I'll hold onto it this time," she said.

As they were leaving the spaceport a huge gust of wind swept past them. Rebekah looked alarmed as it tugged at the comic and blew it away. "You didn't tell me it was alive!" she said. "It isn't," Jasmin replied, looking puzzled.

It had been raining outside. There were puddles everywhere. Rebekah stepped in one and it splashed over her feet. "Oh no, something's moving on my feet!" she said in distress. She switched on her anti-gravity device and floated above the ground. Benny noticed something strange was happening to Rebekah. She was turning pink.

Then it started to rain. "Ughh!" Rebekah exclaimed, turning even more pink. "Something's moving on my head!" Benny tried to explain that it was only rain. Perhaps they didn't have rain on planet Roxolon. By now poor Rebekah was looking very anxious and very pink indeed. "Oh what am I to do? Earth is so frightening. Why do so many things move on their own?"

Jasmin and Benny looked at each other. Helium balloons? Wind? Rain? What was the connection? Then they remembered. No wonder Rebekah was confused. There are no liquids and gases on Roxolon!

Just then Grandad and Millie arrived. Jasmin explained that Rebekah was so frightened that she had turned pink. What could they do to help her to recognise liquids and gases? Everyone thought very hard and then started to talk about their ideas.

Try to think of your own ideas for finding out.
Here are some of our ideas for what you could do...

It would be helpful to find different materials and try to sort them into solids, liquids and gases.

How about finding things that you think might confuse your friends such as:

- ⊚ plasticine
- ⊚ sand ⊚ glue
- ⊚ whipped cream ⊚ tomato puree
- ⊚ hair gel ⊚ tippex, etc.

Decide which groups to put them in, then try them out on your friends.

DO NOT explore coloured gases. They are usually VERY POISONOUS.

Use a scale of 1 to 10 to sort materials.

1 can be a gas like helium and

10 can be a solid like rock.

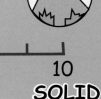

1
GAS

10
SOLID

Your challenge is to see if you can find something for each number.

You could make a guide to solids, liquids and gases to help some one else decide what goes into which group.

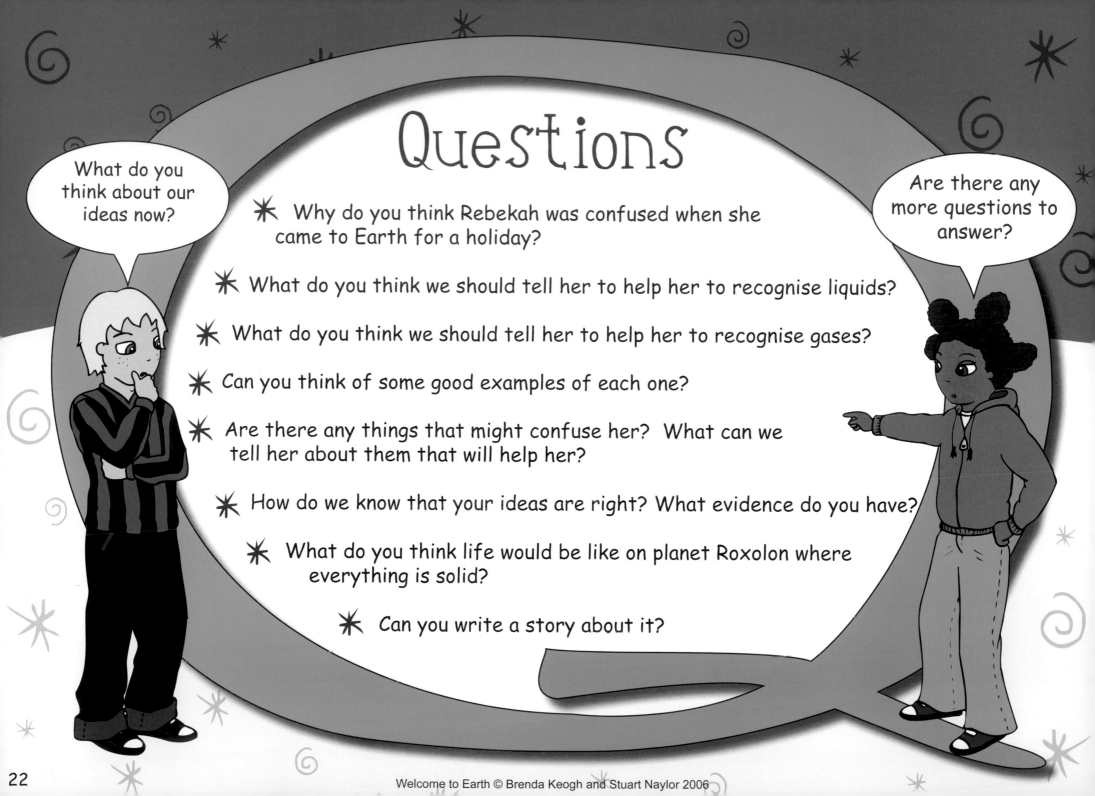

Questions

What do you think about our ideas now?

Are there any more questions to answer?

✳ Why do you think Rebekah was confused when she came to Earth for a holiday?

✳ What do you think we should tell her to help her to recognise liquids?

✳ What do you think we should tell her to help her to recognise gases?

✳ Can you think of some good examples of each one?

✳ Are there any things that might confuse her? What can we tell her about them that will help her?

✳ How do we know that your ideas are right? What evidence do you have?

✳ What do you think life would be like on planet Roxolon where everything is solid?

✳ Can you write a story about it?

The big idea in this story is that materials are often grouped as solids, liquids and gases but things do not always fit neatly into these groups.

The terms solid, liquid and gas help to describe the world around us.

★ Solids will normally keep their shape even without a container.

★ Liquids are normally runny and take the shape of a container.

★ Gases often cannot be seen and flow easily. They are also easier to squash.

In real life things do not always fit into neat groups, for example:

★ Sand and salt are runny like a liquid but they are really lots of tiny solids.

★ Gels do not hold a firm shape like solid blocks of wood but they do not run like liquids. They are somewhere between the two.

★ Whipped cream is a mixture of a liquid (water), solid (fat) and a gas (air).

Gases help us to smell perfume and other odours over long distances.

Different gases are more difficult to find.

• You can see gas burning in fires and cookers.

• Air is made up of lots of different gases.

• You find carbon dioxide bubbles in fizzy drinks.

You can get helium balloons from a party shop.

A Dry Spell

Benny was feeling really miserable. He talked to himself, since nobody was there to hear him. "It's not fair," he said. "I'll be hungry all afternoon. My sandwiches are much too dry to eat now. How would I know that they would get so dried up if I left them out in the sun?"

Benny spotted Little Wizard coming in his direction. He called Little Wizard over. "Hello, Little Wizard. How are you today?" Little Wizard replied, "I'm very well, thank you. And how are you?"

Benny told him that he was fed up. He'd left his sandwiches out and they had dried up in the sun. Little Wizard was sympathetic. He could understand why Benny was fed up but he didn't know if he could help. He was still learning spells and didn't know any spells to fix dried up lunches.

Suddenly Little Wizard's eyes lit up. "I'll tell you what Benny, I could do a spell to stop things drying up. Then it won't matter if you leave your lunch out in future." And without further ado Little Wizard started his spell. Benny looked in amazement at Little Wizard. He thought it was a brilliant spell. That should solve the problem.

Just then Jasmin arrived. Benny couldn't wait to tell her about how Little Wizard had cast a spell to stop the water drying up so that he wouldn't have a problem with his lunch in future.

Jasmin listened carefully. "Let me get this straight. You're saying that Little Wizard has cast a spell to stop water drying up? That's any water, anywhere? And the spell will work all over the Earth?"

Benny and Little Wizard nodded together as Jasmin spoke. Jasmin thought it might not be a good idea. "I think it won't rain anymore. Then the rivers will stop running and nothing will grow in the fields and gardens."

Benny looked confused. What was the problem? The spell was about water drying up, not whether it would rain.

At that point Grandad and Millie arrived. They saw that Benny was looking puzzled. Benny told them about how his lunch had dried up and what Jasmin had said about Little Wizard's spell. Now they were puzzled too. Everyone had different ideas about what might happen.

Try to think of your own ideas for finding out.
Here are some of our ideas for what you could do...

You could observe how wet things change if they are left to dry:

- parts of plants (e.g. flowers)

- moist food (e.g. bread, fruit)

- washing on a line, rain on a coat, water in puddles

How about investigating what helps water to evaporate? Think carefully about how to make sure that your results are accurate.

Can you use your results to decide the best way to make water evaporate quickly?

Why not have a condensation hunt?

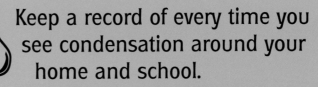

Keep a record of every time you see condensation around your home and school.

Try to work out where and when you should look.

Can you find ways to stop things drying out?

What about doing some research into the rain cycle?

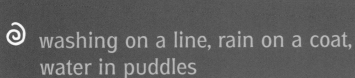

Where would be the best places to look for information?

Questions

* What kinds of things dry up? Can you stop things drying up?

* Where do you think water goes to when it dries up?

* Where do you think the rain comes from?

* How are evaporation and condensation linked with the water cycle?

* Can any water that evaporates anywhere be part of the water cycle?

* What do you think about Little Wizard's spell?

* How do we know your ideas are right? What evidence do you have?

* Why don't you make up some better spells for Little Wizard to stop sandwiches drying up?

28

The big idea in this story is the water cycle. Water evaporates, then condenses to form clouds and falls to earth again as rain.

When water evaporates it becomes water gas that cannot be seen. When it cools it forms water droplets again. We call this condensation.

The same process happens in the bathroom when you are having a bath or shower.

You can see condensation:

★ on a cold mirror   ★ on a very cold drinks can

★ on grass and cars on a cold morning.

Jasmin was right to think that it would not rain any more if Little Wizard had stopped water drying up.

★ It is not only water from the sea that causes the rain.

★ Water that has evaporated anywhere can help to form rain clouds or mist and fog.

★ Even the water from Benny's sandwiches has evaporated into the air.

You can see evaporation and condensation together in a sealed see-through container.

Put some warm water in the bottom. Put a tight cover on the top. Then water will evaporate from the bottom.

As it condenses drops of water will appear on the lid.

This is an invisible process. It is science, not magic!

A Dry Spell © Brenda Keogh and Stuart Naylor 2006

Day and Night

It was a warm summer afternoon. Jasmin and Benny were planning to have a picnic. They were in the field looking for a good place to stop. "Come on Jasmin, we have to stop soon," Benny said. He was carrying the picnic basket and it felt like they had been walking for ages.

"Just a bit further," Jasmin replied. "I can see a good spot over there." They soon had a blanket on the grass and their picnic spread out in front of them.

Jasmin looked around. She watched the fluffy white clouds moving slowly overhead in the bright blue sky. "I love the bright blue sky," Jasmin said. "It's so much better than the dark sky at night."

Benny looked around. He watched a skylark flying overhead. "I love these bright sunny days," Benny said. "They are so much better than dark nights."

There was a flash and Little Wizard suddenly appeared on the blanket. Benny and Jasmin looked surprised. They had forgotten that they had arranged to meet him for the picnic. Fortunately, Little Wizard had brought his magic wand. He waved it in the air and muttered a spell. Instantly a gigantic, wobbly jelly landed at Benny's feet. "Oh!" said Little Wizard "that's not quite what I expected."

The afternoon slipped by while they lazed in the sun, ate the food and talked about some of Little Wizard's latest ideas for spells.

Suddenly Jasmin noticed the Sun was starting to set. She explained to Little Wizard that she didn't like the dark. Benny said that he didn't like the dark either.

"Can you do a spell for us Little Wizard? Can you make it daytime all the time?" asked Jasmin. "Yes, go on Little Wizard," Benny added. "Do a spell to turn night into day."

Little Wizard looked uncertain. "I don't know any spells to turn night into day," he said. "But I could do one to stop things moving. I could cast a spell to stop the Sun moving in the sky, so it would always be daytime."

Just then Grandad and Millie arrived. They overheard Little Wizard's idea for the spell to stop the Sun moving in the sky. Everyone started to talk about whether the spell could make it daytime all the time.

Try to think of your own ideas for finding out.
Here are some of our ideas for what you could do...

Books and the internet could help you to find out more about day and night. You could look at videos and CD-ROMS too.

Why not visit a space centre or look at its website? What can it tell you about day and night?

You could make a model with a bright light for the Sun and a ball for the Earth.

Put a dot on the ball (Earth) for where you live.

DO NOT look directly at the Sun

What do you need to do to the 'Earth' to get the dot to go into the darkness and then into the light?

If you tilt the model Earth towards and away from the model Sun, does it make a difference?

What happens when you tilt the model Earth TOWARDS the model Sun?

What happens when you tilt the model Earth AWAY from the model Sun?

Observe what happens to the amount of time the dot is in the light.

What happens at the equator?

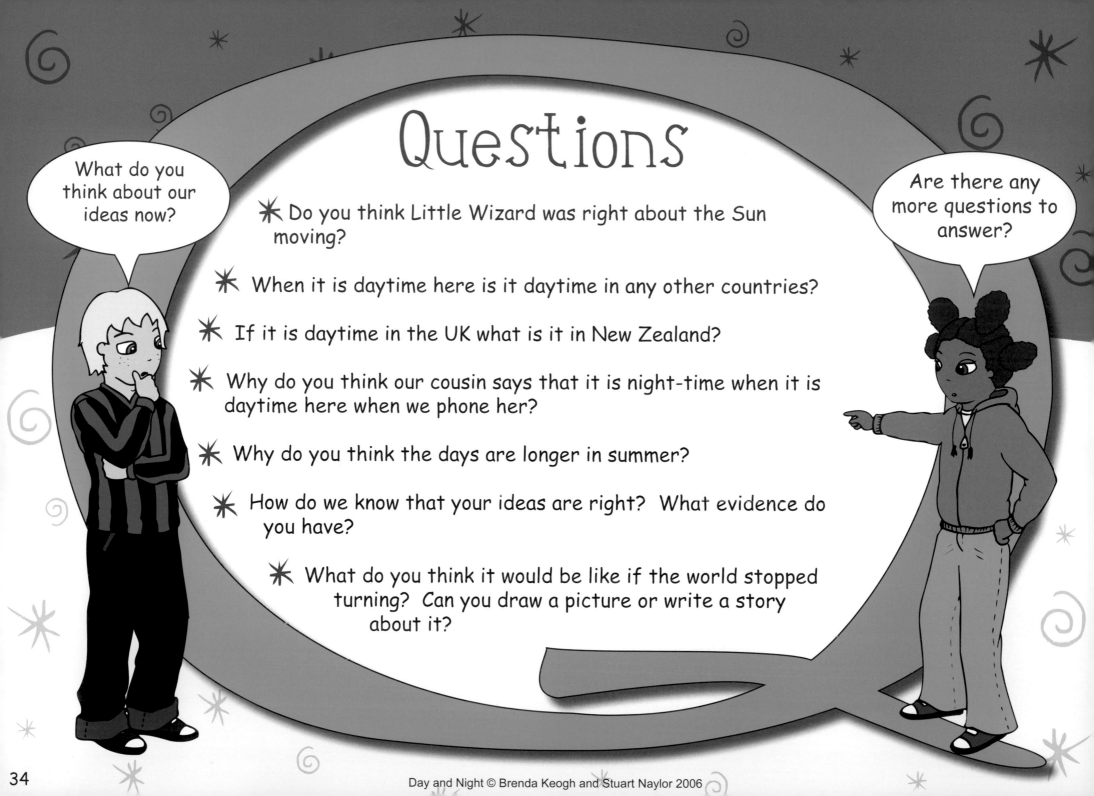

Questions

What do you think about our ideas now?

Are there any more questions to answer?

✳ Do you think Little Wizard was right about the Sun moving?

✳ When it is daytime here is it daytime in any other countries?

✳ If it is daytime in the UK what is it in New Zealand?

✳ Why do you think our cousin says that it is night-time when it is daytime here when we phone her?

✳ Why do you think the days are longer in summer?

✳ How do we know that your ideas are right? What evidence do you have?

✳ What do you think it would be like if the world stopped turning? Can you draw a picture or write a story about it?

The big idea in this story is that day and night happen because the Earth moves, not the Sun. Day length changes because the Earth's axis is at an angle to the Sun.

Day and night happen because the Earth spins round on its axis once every 24 hours.

★ When the side of the Earth you live on faces the Sun it is daylight.

★ When it faces away from the Sun it is night.

The Sun looks as if it moves across the sky during the day but it is really the Earth that is turning.

★ As the Earth turns you can see the planets and stars move across the sky each night.

★ The Earth is also orbiting the Sun (our star).

★ The other planets orbit the Sun. They are all in our solar system.

★ The other stars are like our Sun but far away.

Have you noticed that there is more daylight in the summer than in the winter?

The Earth's axis is at an angle to the Sun. On the equator it goes dark at about the same time every day. The angle to the Sun is almost the same all year.

In summer the part you live on leans towards the Sun. Days are longer and nights are shorter.

In winter the part you live on leans away from the Sun. Days are shorter and nights are longer.

Day and Night © Brenda Keogh and Stuart Naylor 2006

35

Noisy Neighbours

Ronald Rat lay in bed and held his head in his hands. It was impossible. He just couldn't get to sleep. He was getting more tired and more irritable each day. The sound of crashes, bangs and screeches came through the wall.

It was followed by loud music. He could hear guitars, drums and squeaky singing. Then there was a barrage of tiny footsteps running up and downstairs next door.

Ronald Rat groaned out loud. "Why did they have to move in next door to me? There are 18 of them! They're so noisy! I don't know what I am going to do." So Ronald Rat turned over, pulled the bedclothes over his head and tried to get some sleep.

The next day Minelli Mole came to visit. After their tea and cake they played some sports. Minelli Mole always won if they played burrowing.

Ronald Rat always won if they played computer games because Minelli Mole couldn't see the screen properly.

Today Minelli Mole looked a bit concerned. She said that Ronald was looking a bit tired. She asked him if anything was bothering him. Ronald Rat explained that there were 18 things bothering him, and they all lived next door!

Minelli Mole asked Ronald if he had tried aluminium foil on the walls. She said that one of her friends tried it on his tunnel when he had some building work done, and he's sure that it kept the sound out.

Ronald Rat looked extremely doubtful. He wanted to know if she meant the same kind of aluminium foil that he uses to wrap his sandwiches. He thought it was much too thin to keep the noise out.

At that point Jasmin and Benny arrived to join them for tea and cake. Ronald Rat asked them for help with his problem. Jasmin said that they should talk to Grandad and Millie because they were good at thinking about ideas when there was a problem to solve.

When Grandad and Millie arrived Jasmin explained the problem to them. They all began to talk about their ideas.

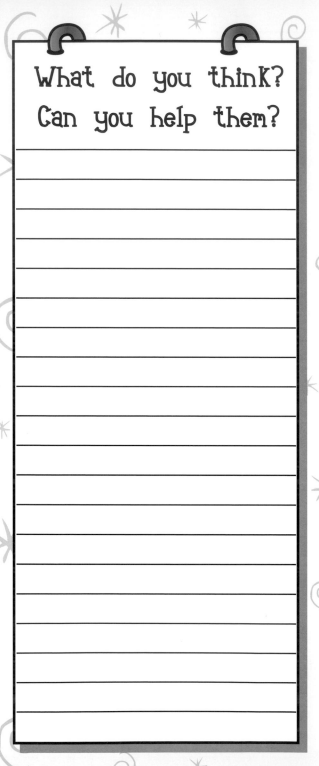

Try to think of your own ideas for finding out.
Here are some of our ideas for what you could do...

You could explore what happens when you wrap materials around a noisy object.

- 🌀 Which is the best at stopping the sound coming through?

- 🌀 Have a vote on all the materials – good, quite good and useless.

- 🌀 Do you agree with each other?

- 🌀 Do you need to do a fair test to check any of your ideas?

How about finding out if materials that conduct sound also conduct heat?

Here's one way that you could test your ideas more systematically.

Put a noisy object (such as an alarm clock, a buzzer or a radio) into a box and fill the space around it with the material you want to try. Listen to the difference with and without the materials. How can you make sure you are testing all the materials in the same way?

Do you have a sound meter or datalogger?

You could use this to measure the sound levels. This is the most accurate way to find out which materials work best. You can use a computer to make a record of the results.

Questions

✳ What do you think about Minelli Mole's idea? What do you know of that can stop sound? Is foil a good idea?

✳ Can you hear some types of sound better than others?

✳ Millie talked about conductors. Do you think she meant a conductor of an orchestra so that the noise from the mice would sound better?

✳ We thought you wrap insulators round things to keep them warm. What do you think a sound insulator might do?

✳ We had double-glazing put in our house. We can't hear the sound of the ice cream van in the street any more. Why do you think that is?

✳ How do we know that your ideas are right? What evidence do you have?

✳ Why don't you write a letter to tell Ronald what to do?

The big idea in this story is sound insulation. Some materials can affect the way that sounds travel and stop the sound waves reaching your ear.

Soft materials do not conduct sound as easily as hard materials

★ The thicker the material the better it should be at stopping sound.

★ Metal and wood conduct sound but a thick layer could block the sound waves and help to reduce the noise.

★ A thin layer of foil on its own will not help Ronald.

Sound does not travel as easily though trapped air

★ Double glazing uses air trapped between two panes of glass to help to reduce noise.

★ Materials such as cotton wool, bubble wrap or sponge have air trapped inthem. They could help to reduce the noise.

★ Building an extra wall to create an air gap between his house and the house next door could also help Ronald.

Benny and Jasmin need to make sure that they do not get confused between different types of conductors. Metals can conduct heat and sound . Wood is different. It conducts sound. But it does not conduct heat well. This is why it is used for handles on pans.

Fox and Hens

It was a crisp sunny morning. Jasmin was outside in the garden, putting out food for the birds. Benny came to join Jasmin in the garden. He had run to the shop to get bread and milk for breakfast.

Benny looked at Jasmin putting food out for the birds. "I'm hungry too," he said. "In fact I'm starving. What else are we having for breakfast?" Jasmin didn't reply. She set off across the garden. Benny realised where she was going and followed her. "Eggs!" Benny thought. "New laid eggs! Fantastic!" There was nothing better for breakfast than new laid eggs.

As they reached the hen run they could both see that something wasn't right. There were feathers everywhere. "Benny, what's happened?" Jasmin wailed, pointing into the hen run. Benny looked into the hen run. "Some of the hens are missing. There should be more hens than this."

At that point Little Wizard appeared. He often came round for an early morning cup of tea. He looked at the feathers on the ground.

"It will be the fox," Little Wizard said. "I've seen it prowling round here early in the morning. Look, you can see a hole in the wire netting where it must have found a way in."

"That fox!" Jasmin shouted. "Wait till I see it! Can you do a spell to fix it, Little Wizard? You must know a spell to stop the fox getting at our hens." "Well, not exactly," Little Wizard explained. "I don't know any spells for foxes. But I do know one for what animals eat. I could cast a spell to stop animals eating other animals and make them eat plants instead. Look here it is." Little Wizard then told Jasmin and Benny his spell.

Jasmin looked pleased. "Brilliant. That should fix it. What are you waiting for Little Wizard?" Little Wizard thought hard in a wizardly way. Then in a flash he went to find his magic wand.

By now Benny was looking doubtful. He saw that Grandad and Millie had arrived, so he called them over to tell them what had happened and about Little Wizard's idea for a spell. They all started to talk about the spell and whether it would stop the fox taking the hens in future.

What do you think?
Can you help them?

Try to think of your own ideas for finding out.
Here are some of our ideas for what you could do...

You could use books or the internet to find out about the difference between carnivores and herbivores.

You can think about how animals survive by being part of food chains.

Which food chains include a fox?

What would happen if one of the animals or plants in a food chain died out?

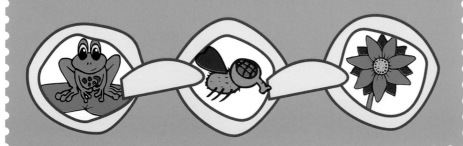

What would happen to the number of mice if there were no predators?

If a pair of mice has 10 babies every 3 months, how many babies will they have in a year if none were eaten by predators?

What would happen if every new pair of mice also had 10 babies once every three months after they were born?

If every mouse ate 10g of food per day how much food would they all need in one day or one year?

How many 1kg bags of cereal would that be?

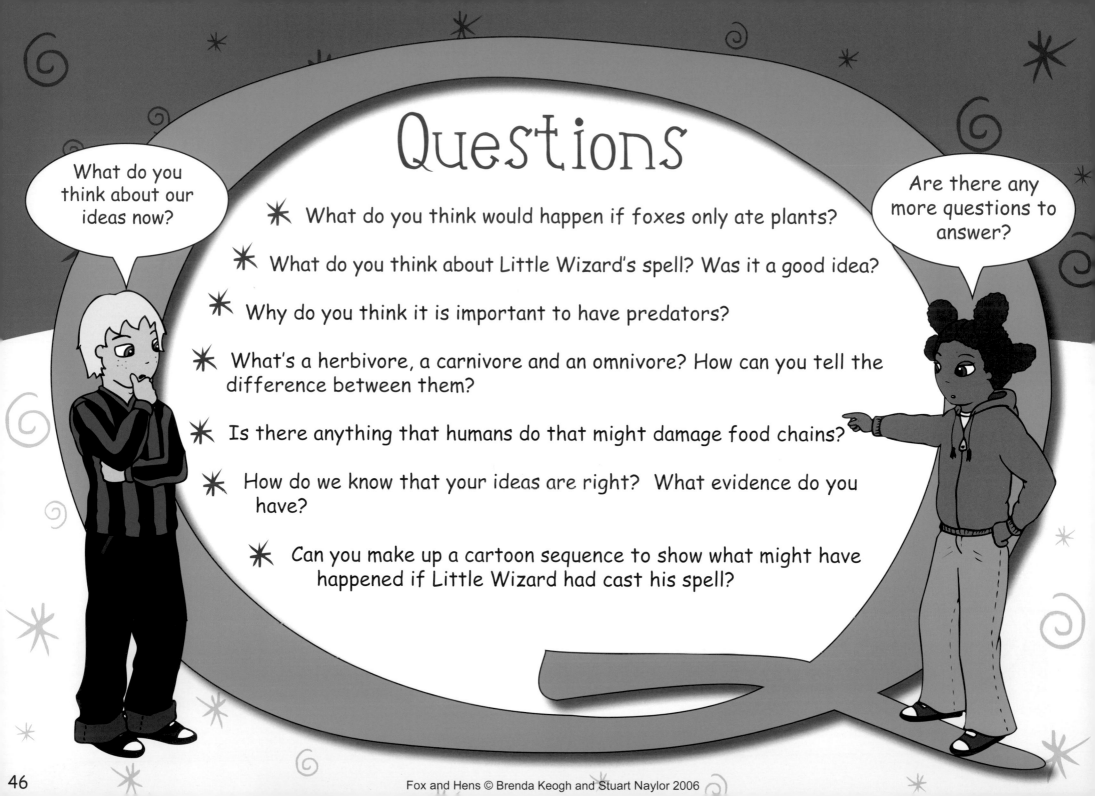

Questions

What do you think about our ideas now?

Are there any more questions to answer?

※ What do you think would happen if foxes only ate plants?

※ What do you think about Little Wizard's spell? Was it a good idea?

※ Why do you think it is important to have predators?

※ What's a herbivore, a carnivore and an omnivore? How can you tell the difference between them?

※ Is there anything that humans do that might damage food chains?

※ How do we know that your ideas are right? What evidence do you have?

※ Can you make up a cartoon sequence to show what might have happened if Little Wizard had cast his spell?

The big idea in this story is that meat eating and plant eating animals are linked together in food chains. Food chains are connected to form food webs.

Plants and animals living in an area or habitat need to stay in balance to survive.

Think about foxes, rabbits and plants in a simple food chain.

 Plants

ARE EATEN BY

 Rabbits

ARE EATEN BY

 Foxes

Little Wizard's spell would mean that animals could only eat plants.

★ Eventually all the plants would be eaten and the animals would starve.

★ Some animals would find plants hard to eat as they are adapted to survive as carnivores. Imagine a lion only eating grass!

★ Diseases and human activity can have a serious impact on animal populations in food chains.

If there are:

• too many foxes and not enough rabbits then eventually some of the foxes could starve.

• too many rabbits and not enough foxes then the rabbit population will grow. The rabbits could eat all the plants available and they could starve.

Jasmin and Benny need to realise that foxes eating other animals is normal behaviour.

Foxes are adapted to eat meat. Little Wizard needs to help to make the hen run fox-proof!

Food in the Fridge

Jasmin and Benny went to the market together. They had a list of things to buy. They had been given twenty pounds and told not to waste it on crisps and sweets.

It was an old-fashioned market. The kind of market that has stalls in the street, with canvas canopies to keep the food dry when it rains and shade it from the sun in the summer. It was the first time that Jasmin and Benny had been to the market on their own. They were feeling very responsible.

"Look at these Jasmin!" Benny shouted. "Why would anybody buy these? They are all brown and wrinkly. They look disgusting!" Jasmin explained that they were passion fruits and although they looked horrible they tasted fantastic. Fruit was on the shopping list, so she bought some to take home.

Benny wanted to get some bananas and mangos as well, so they could make fruit smoothies. Grandad had shown him how to make fruit smoothies. They were really easy to make and they tasted brilliant.

Jasmin and Benny carried on round the market. They bought fruit, vegetables, fish, bread and meat. No crisps or sweets – but they did buy two ice cream cones instead.

When they got back they unpacked the food in the kitchen. Benny opened the fridge. It was nearly full. There wasn't room for all the food. He put the fruit in the space that was left in the fridge.

Jasmin took the fruit out of the fridge and put the meat in its place. "What are you doing?" Benny asked. "I like cold fruit smoothies. They taste better cold."

Jasmin sighed, "The meat has to go in the fridge or invisible microbes will make it go bad."

"Invisible microbes?" Benny grumbled. "I can't see any. If there are microbes won't they still be on the meat in the fridge? Will the fruit have microbes as well?" Benny obviously didn't think much of Jasmin's idea. Jasmin shut the fridge door firmly. She told Benny that she wasn't making it up.

Grandad and Millie arrived to help unpack the shopping. Jasmin explained that they were arguing about which food had to go in the fridge.

They all began to think about microbes and food. Then everyone started talking about their ideas.

Try to think of your own ideas for finding out.
Here are some of our ideas for what you could do...

CHECK WITH AN ADULT

Why not use websites and books to find out about microbes on food?

- Are there different kinds of microbes?

- Where do you find them?

- Are there helpful and harmful microbes?

DO NOT use meat or fish in your investigations. Remember to wash your hands.

You could investigate microbes on food.

Put small bits of moist food such as bread, cheese and fruit in well-sealed bags.

Keep them in warm and cold places.

How many different ways can you find to preserve food without a fridge?

Why not draw, photograph or note what happens to the food?

Ask people who work with food what they have to do to make sure that food is safe to eat.

 Do not open the bags or touch the ROTTING food.

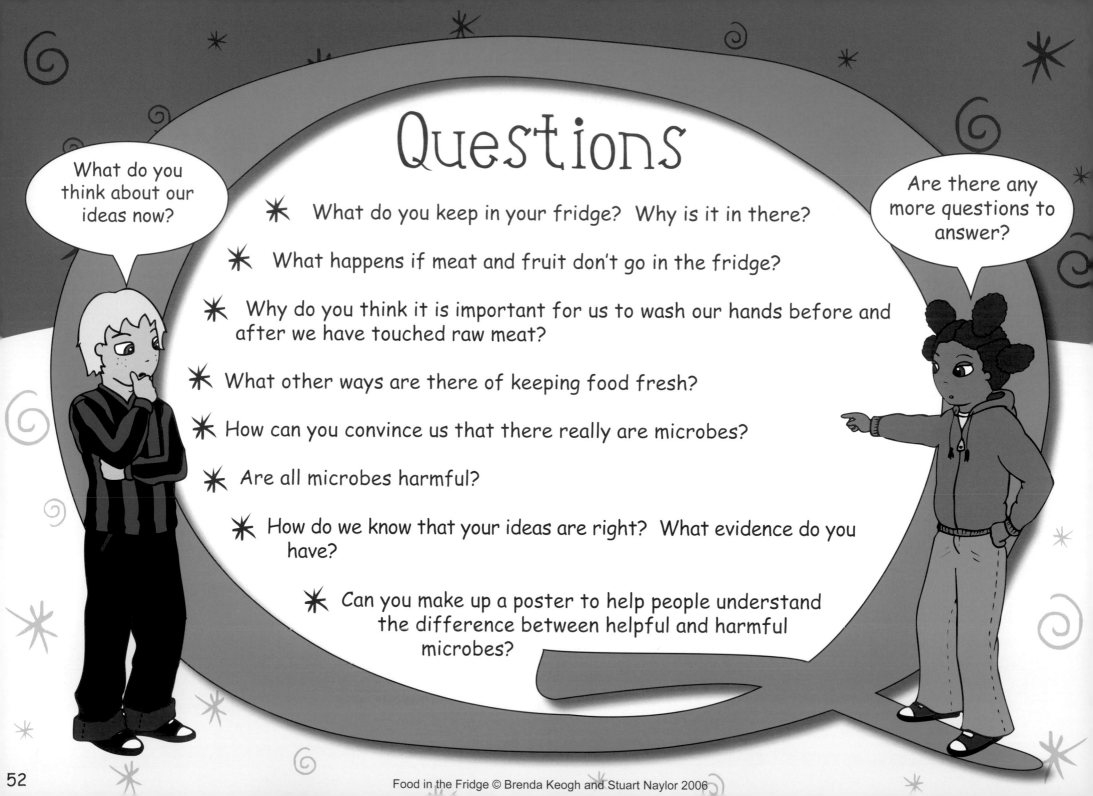

Questions

* What do you keep in your fridge? Why is it in there?

* What happens if meat and fruit don't go in the fridge?

* Why do you think it is important for us to wash our hands before and after we have touched raw meat?

* What other ways are there of keeping food fresh?

* How can you convince us that there really are microbes?

* Are all microbes harmful?

* How do we know that your ideas are right? What evidence do you have?

* Can you make up a poster to help people understand the difference between helpful and harmful microbes?

What do you think about our ideas now?

Are there any more questions to answer?

The big idea in this story is that there are invisible microbes all around us. Normally they are not harmful but sometimes they can make you very ill.

Grandad is right, there are microbes all around us.

★ A microbe is a tiny living organism. There are different types such as fungi and bacteria.

★ Microbe is short for micro-organism, which means small organism.

★ They can be seen through very powerful microscopes.

There are many kinds of microbes.

★ We use them to make bread, yogurt, and to rot down waste.

★ Harmful microbes multiply quickly on fresh foods, particularly meat, poultry, fish and dairy products.

★ Microbes multiply more easily once fruit is peeled and pureed.

★ Putting food in the fridge slows down the growth of microbes.

All food will eventually rot because of microbes. Here are some of the ways you can preserve food:

• freezing it   • pickling it

• making it into jam   • drying it

• sealing it in airtight containers

• smoking it

• putting salt on it

• canning it

Mister Miser

Mr Miser sat back in his chair and rubbed his hands. He glanced out of the window at the enormous tanks in his garden. A smile came over his face. He was thinking of how much salt he had in his tanks.

"Another fantastic bargain!" he thought to himself. "I saved lots of money when I bought really cheap candles. So what if they don't have wicks? I'm sure I can make them light. Then I bought cut-price pencils. So what if they are leadless? I'm sure I can make them write. And now I've bought heaps of salt. So what if it is rock salt? I'm sure it will taste good on my fish and chips. I'm just so brilliant."

So Mr Miser made himself a cup of tea, watched the news on the television and read for a while. He sat contentedly in his chair and started to doze. He was very satisfied with himself. Suddenly a loud noise woke him up. He wondered what the noise was. Then he realised it was only thunder and lightning, so he sat back in his chair and ignored the rest of the storm.

The following morning Jasmin and Benny were walking to catch the bus to school. They passed Mr Miser's house on their way to the bus stop. "What's wrong, Mr Miser?" Jasmin called out. She could see Mr Miser in tears in his garden.

"My salt. My precious store of salt. What's happened to my salt?" he moaned. He was very agitated. "What salt?" Benny asked. "I can't see any salt."

"That's the whole point! There isn't any! It's gone! Vanished! Disappeared! I was storing it to put on my fish and chips. What will I do now?" Mr Miser peered into the tank and looked really upset.

Jasmin walked over, stood on tiptoe and looked inside the tank. All she could see was a big pool of what looked like water. She tried to remember what she knew about salt and water. "Have a look Benny," she said. "I can't see any salt. Can you?" Benny looked into the tank as well. He couldn't see any salt either.

"Well you two aren't much use," Mr Miser grumbled. "How am I going to get my salt back?"

Jasmin saw Grandad and Millie passing so she called them over. They usually had good ideas when there was a problem. Jasmin explained the problem to them. They all started to think about how they could get the salt back.

Try to think of your own ideas for finding out. Here are some of our ideas for what you could do...

CHECK WITH AN ADULT

You could have fun exploring what happens when you mix different things with water, for example: salt, sugar, flour, cornflour, coloured sugar crystals.

How about trying to get the salt out of salty water? For example:

- leave it in a saucer in cold and hot places.

- heat the salty water in a metal tray over a tea light.

- leave some in a bowl in a sunny spot.

Look for photographs of people in various parts of the world collecting salt from seawater.

DO NOT taste to see if salt or sugar is in the water.

You could investigate your questions about dissolving and evaporating.

- Does more of the substance dissolve if the water is hotter?

- Does stirring make it worse or better?

- Does heating speed up evaporation?

- How could you make sure that your tests are fair?

Find out about brine springs, salt panning and salt mining.

Visit the Northwich Salt Museum's Web Site www.saltmuseum.org.uk.

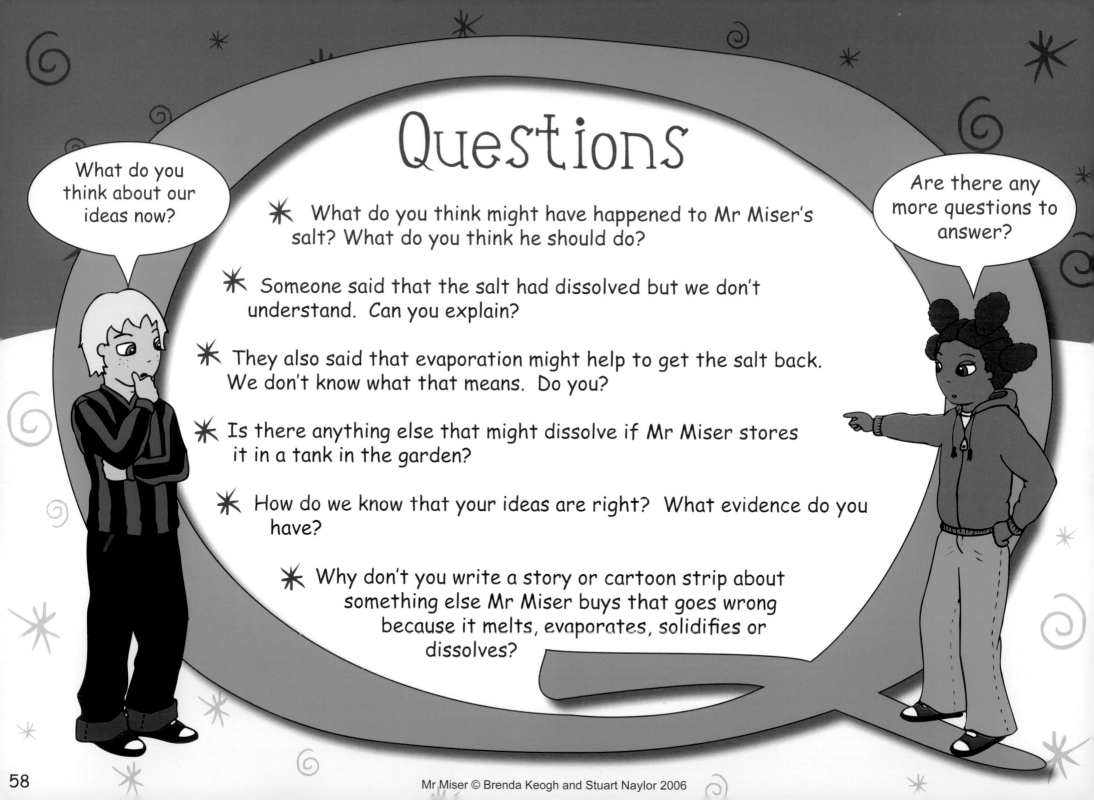

Questions

What do you think about our ideas now?

Are there any more questions to answer?

* What do you think might have happened to Mr Miser's salt? What do you think he should do?

* Someone said that the salt had dissolved but we don't understand. Can you explain?

* They also said that evaporation might help to get the salt back. We don't know what that means. Do you?

* Is there anything else that might dissolve if Mr Miser stores it in a tank in the garden?

* How do we know that your ideas are right? What evidence do you have?

* Why don't you write a story or cartoon strip about something else Mr Miser buys that goes wrong because it melts, evaporates, solidifies or dissolves?

The big idea in this story is that some substances dissolve in water. Evaporation can be used to get the substance back.

When things dissolve in water it may look as if they have disappeared.

This is what Mr Miser thinks. He is wrong. His salt is still there but he just cannot see it.

★ He needs to use evaporation to get his salt back.

★ Heating helps liquids to evaporate, and can help substances to dissolve faster.

People use evaporation to get salt from seawater or brine springs.

★ They heat up the water in big flat pans or

★ leave the water to dry out in pools.

★ When the water has gone they are left with salt crystals.

★ Brine is another name for very salty water.

Not everything dissolves in water.

Powders such as flour mix with the water but if you leave it the powder drops to the bottom of the container. The powder has not dissolved.

Disappearing Candle

"This is hopeless!" Benny said. "I can't read with just a candle." He shut his book firmly and looked irritated. "We just have to put up with it Benny," said Jasmin. She sat quietly by the candle, watching the flame. "Why don't you go and play a video game? Or listen to some music?"

Benny looked at Jasmin. He was irritated with her as well. He reminded her that there was a power cut. They didn't have any electricity. He couldn't use his video game. Or his music system. Or his computer. "Sorry Benny, of course you can't. What about making us a fruit smoothie . . ." Jasmin's voice tailed off as she realised that Benny couldn't use the electric blender to make a fruit smoothie either.

Then Jasmin had an idea. She explained to Benny that the candle is really interesting if you watch it carefully. She told him to have a look at the flame. Benny looked at the candle flame closely. Actually it was really interesting! The flame was all sorts of colours and shapes. It made some fascinating patterns.

Benny started to describe to Jasmin what he could see. He pointed to the wax melting at the top of the candle where it's hottest. He noticed that the flame doesn't start at the bottom of the wick – it starts part way up. He wondered why that was.

"I haven't a clue," said Jasmin. "I only said it was interesting. I didn't say that I understand how it works." So they looked at the candle flame together for a few minutes.

"I'll tell you what, Benny," Jasmin said, "this reminds me of water. You know how ice melts and turns into water, then the water evaporates and turns into water vapour. Well I think the wax is just like that. I think it's melting and then evaporating!" "Wow," said Benny. "If it's like water then we should be able to get the wax back again. We can burn the candle in a jar, and the wax vapour will condense into little drops of wax, just like water condenses. Then we can make some new candles!"

Jasmin looked doubtful. At that point Grandad and Millie came into the room. Benny explained how they were wondering about the candle. Was the wax really like water? Everyone looked very closely at the candle then started to talk about their ideas.

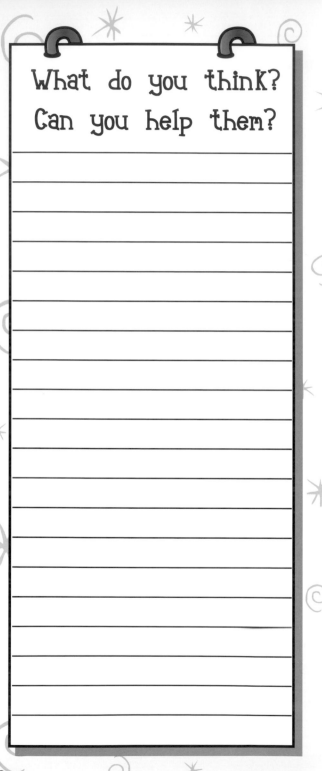

Disappearing Candle © Brenda Keogh and Stuart Naylor 2006

Try to think of your own ideas for finding out.
Here are some of our ideas for what you could do...

CHECK WITH AN ADULT

It's fascinating watching a candle burning. You could draw a picture of what you can see.

Why not try collecting anything that comes from a burning candle?

Put a large jar over the candle.

Leave it until the flame goes out.

Is there wax on the inside of the jar?

Can you see anything else in the jar?

Don't heat anything you're not sure is safe. Plastics, rubber and some liquids can be very dangerous. Loose clothes and hair should be tied back.

How about exploring what happens when you heat or burn things?

Start by gently heating wax.

Is it the same as the burning candle?

Try other things like paper, wood, chocolate and water.

Make a note of which of them melt, evaporate or burn.

Make a chart to record your results.

Use tea lights in sand for heating, they are much safer than candles.

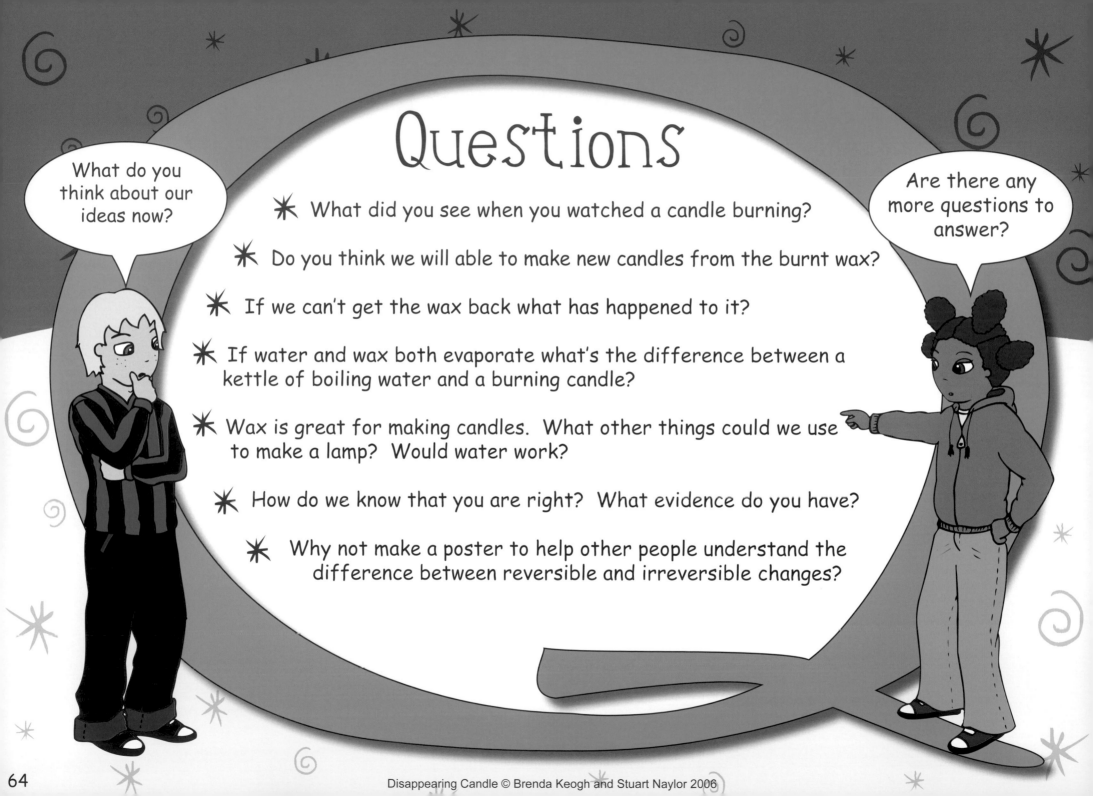

Questions

* What did you see when you watched a candle burning?

* Do you think we will able to make new candles from the burnt wax?

* If we can't get the wax back what has happened to it?

* If water and wax both evaporate what's the difference between a kettle of boiling water and a burning candle?

* Wax is great for making candles. What other things could we use to make a lamp? Would water work?

* How do we know that you are right? What evidence do you have?

* Why not make a poster to help other people understand the difference between reversible and irreversible changes?

What do you think about our ideas now?

Are there any more questions to answer?

The big idea in this story is that things change when they are heated. Sometimes the changes can be reversed and sometimes they cannot.

When candle wax burns you cannot get all the wax back. It is an irreversible change.

★ Solid wax melts when it is heated.

★ The melted wax goes up the wick.

★ As it gets hotter it evaporates and it becomes wax gas or vapour.

★ The flame is the vapour burning.

H
=
Hydrogen

O
=
Oxygen

C
=
Carbon

When things burn in air they change.

★ Wax is mostly hydrogen and carbon particles .

★ When candles burn, oxygen in the air joins with the hydrogen to form water (H_2O).

★ Oxygen also joins with the carbon to make a gas called carbon dioxide (CO_2).

★ You can get carbon (black soot) on its own too.

★ You can see the carbon and water if you catch it in a jar.

Water does not burn when it evaporates. It is a reversible change.

When wood and paper burn they change into things like carbon, carbon dioxide and water. This is an irreversible change.

If wax and chocolate only melt, they will solidify again. It is a reversible change.

CO_2 is a good fire extinguisher. It helps to put out the candle's flame in the jar.

Bungee Jumpers © Brenda Keogh and Stuart Naylor 2006

Bungee Jumpers

Jasmin took a deep breath and shuffled her feet nervously. "OK Benny, I'm ready," she shouted. "Right Jasmin, the camera is set up," Benny shouted back. Jasmin took another deep breath, shut her eyes and jumped.

"Aaaiiiyyyeee!" she shouted as she fell. She seemed to come down so quickly that there was hardly any time to open her eyes. Suddenly she found that she was going back up in the air! "Aaaiiiyyyeee!" she shouted as she came back down again. She bounced and bounced at the end of the rope until she stopped. "Wow!" she thought. "I've done it! I've done a real bungee jump!"

In no time at all Jasmin was at the bottom of the bungee jumping tower, getting her breath back. Benny checked that she was all right.

"That was great," he said. "I think I got some good pictures as you fell. You came down really quickly," Benny continued. "I don't want to come down any faster than that, but I'm bigger than you so I'll probably fall faster."

"Are you sure Benny?" Jasmin asked. "I'm not sure that it will make any difference."

"It's obvious, isn't it?" Benny replied. "Heavy things will fall faster than light things. I bet Little Wizard can help us." He had seen that Little Wizard was watching the bungee jumpers too.

"Hello Little Wizard," he said. "Can you do a spell for us so that I won't come down too quickly?" "I would be delighted," replied Little Wizard. "I don't know any spells for falling slowly, but I'm sure I can find a suitable one. I've got my Big Book of Spells with me." Little Wizard stared at his Big Book of Spells. He seemed very uncertain about which spell to cast.

Just then Grandad and Millie came over to join them. Grandad had been meaning to ask Little Wizard about a spell to make his hair grow back.

They all started to talk about what kind of spell would be best to make Benny fall slowly.

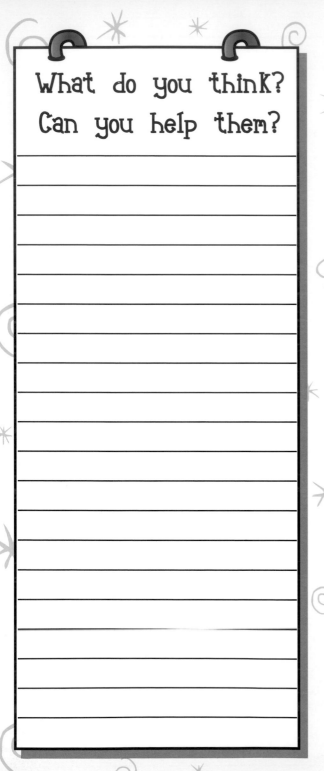

Try to think of your own ideas for finding out.
Here are some of our ideas for what you could do...

Have fun exploring what makes things fall quickly and slowly. Try balls, feathers, paper, dandelion seeds, sycamore seeds. .... Think of questions to answer as you observe the way that things fall.

DO NOT use heavy weights for your bungee jumpers. Be careful not to stretch the elastic too far or it may flick back and hit people.

Here's some questions to think about:

- Do all the people fall at the same speed?

- Does the size or the shape of the person make any difference?

- What happens if you change the elastic?

You could make model bungee jumpers and investigate them falling.

Make the drop as long as possible.

Attach different sized play-people or plasticine people to long pieces of elastic.

Explore what happens first. You might need to do a fair test to answer your questions.

Record your results on a chart.

Explore ways to slow down your bungee jumpers.

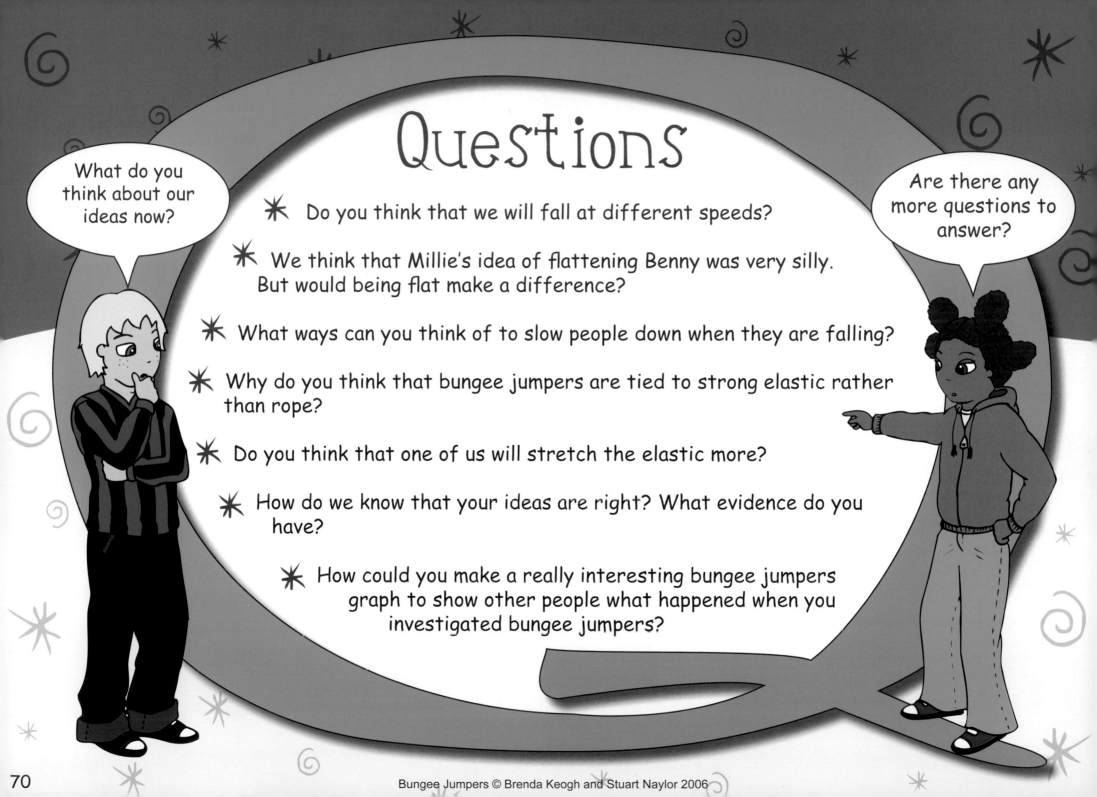

The big ideas in this story are gravity and air resistance and the effect that these have on things that are falling through air.

Benny and Jasmin will fall at the same speed.

★ You might find this hard to believe.

★ Look very carefully and you will see what happens.

★ Even though Benny is heavier, without something to slow him down, gravity will have the same effect on both of them.

The best way to slow something down is to make use of air resistance. This is how parachutes work.

★ Parachutes push against the air and the air pushes back.

★ This makes the person fall more slowly.

★ Flattening Benny might slow him down but wouldn't really do him a lot of good!

Benny will stretch the elastic further than Jasmin.

So Benny doesn't need to worry because he will not fall faster than Jasmin...

This is why bungee jumpers use different thicknesses of elastic. If they all had the same type of elastic the heavy people might hit the ground or the very light people might not bounce much at all!

But he does need to make sure the elastic is strong enough to stop him hitting the ground!

72

Cats in the Dark

Strider and Jim belong to Jasmin and Benny. Strider has a silky soft white coat and his eyes are brilliant yellow. He is the smartest cat in the neighbourhood. Jim has shiny black fur. He is older and wiser than Strider. He can't be bothered chasing mice and his favourite pastime is soaking up sunshine.

Strider and Jim paused outside the park. There were no dogs to be seen. So they meowed to each other and strolled through the park gate and down the path.

As it got dark Jasmin started to get worried. The cats were usually home before this. Where could they be? She decided to go to the park to look for them there. Benny arrived at the park a few minutes later. He was worried too. He couldn't remember the last time they had stayed out this late.

Benny opened his mobile phone. "Should we phone the Animal Rescue to report them missing?" he asked. Jasmin looked doubtful. "It's too early to phone anybody," she replied. "We ought to look for them first."

Benny pointed into the park. He was keen to do something. "Let's go and look for them." Benny went into the park and Jasmin followed. "It's a pity we don't have a torch," he said. "It's almost dark and there aren't any lights in the park." Jasmin looked at Benny. "A torch? We don't need a torch to find them. Their eyes glow in the dark, so we'll see them better without a torch."

Benny shook his head. "I think it will be really hard to spot them without a torch," he said. Now Jasmin shook her head. "It's only at night that you see a cat's eyes glowing," she replied. "And anyway Strider has a white coat too."

Jasmin and Benny looked at each other. Now there were two problems to solve. Strider and Jim were still missing, but would they need a torch to find the cats? At that point Grandad and Millie arrived. Benny explained that Strider and Jim were missing but they couldn't decide whether they would need a torch to find the missing cats. They all started to talk about the best way to see the cats in the dark.

Try to think of your own ideas for finding out. Here are some of our ideas for what you could do...

CHECK WITH AN ADULT

You could have a look at cats in the dark.

- Find a space where you can block out all the light.

- Start with a light on and then use a smaller light such as a torch.

- Switch all the lights off so there is no light at all. What do you see each time?

Perhaps you could get someone with cats to make a video for you.

Film the eyes as well as the fur. If they have night-vision on their camcorder they could try it switched on and off.

Cats MUST be treated with care. Check if anyone is allergic to cat hair.

How about watching out for cats on dark nights? What makes a difference to what you see?

How about looking at different objects in the dark and light?

Choose things that you think you might see in the dark such as:

- a white furry toy
- a mirror
- a bike reflector
- a CD
- aluminium foil
- a coin

How well do you see them in different amounts of light?

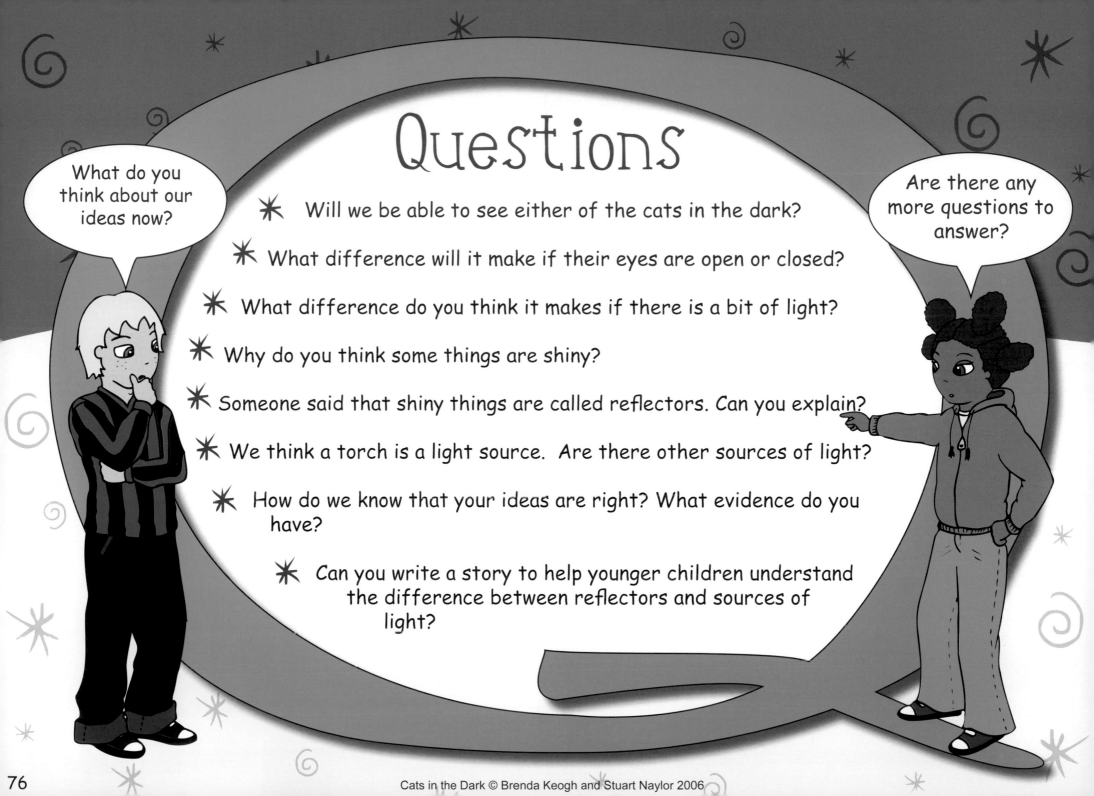

Questions

* Will we be able to see either of the cats in the dark?

* What difference will it make if their eyes are open or closed?

* What difference do you think it makes if there is a bit of light?

* Why do you think some things are shiny?

* Someone said that shiny things are called reflectors. Can you explain?

* We think a torch is a light source. Are there other sources of light?

* How do we know that your ideas are right? What evidence do you have?

* Can you write a story to help younger children understand the difference between reflectors and sources of light?

What do you think about our ideas now?

Are there any more questions to answer?

The big idea in this story is that things that reflect light cannot be seen in complete darkness. Only sources of light can be seen in complete darkness.

It is easy to see why Benny and Jasmin are confused.

★ They are likely to have seen the cats' eyes shining at night.

★ We are told to wear white clothing to be seen at night.

★ Does this mean if it is completely dark we will see Strider's and Jim's eyes and Strider's white coat? No it doesn't!

We only see cats' eyes when a light shines on them from a torch or a car's headlights.

★ White is easier to see than black because it reflects more light.

★ If there is no light at all then Benny and Jasmin will not see either cat.

White fur and cats' eyes are not sources of light.
Nor are other shiny things like foil or a mirror.
They are light reflectors. We can see a torch or a luminous watch when it is dark because they are light sources. Benny and Jasmin will need a torch.

The Lighthouse

Benny and Jasmin sat on the floor next to the lighthouse that they were making. Benny had made a thin metal frame for the top of the lighthouse. "I'll hold the frame in position, and you put the cling film round it," he explained to Jasmin. It was proving rather difficult.

As he held the frame Jasmin held the cling film. She carefully stretched cling film around the frame. "Right Benny, I've got it." Jasmin fastened the end of the cling film so that it didn't unravel. All they needed to do now was to make the lighthouse shine. "Benny, can you get the battery please?" asked Jasmin.

Benny picked up the battery. He attached it carefully to the ends of the wires. Then Jasmin and Benny both leaned back to look at their lighthouse. It was looking pretty impressive. "OK, I think we're ready. Go!" Benny looked at Jasmin to see if she was ready.

Jasmin flipped the switch. She and Benny looked expectantly at the light at the top of their lighthouse. "Is that it? That's pathetic!" Benny exclaimed. He looked really disappointed.

Jasmin looked at the dim light on the top of their lighthouse. "It's not very bright, is it?" she asked, not needing an answer to her question.

"After we worked so hard to make it." She was disappointed too. "Well, I'm not giving up now. We must be able to make it brighter." Benny said. He thought hard for a minute. "We could use extra wires from the battery to the lamp. That should make it brighter."

Jasmin pulled a face. "We don't need extra wires. We need shorter wires to make the lamp brighter."

Benny looked uncertain. "But extra wires can carry more electricity to the lamp, so it will be brighter."

"I'm not sure," replied Jasmin. "If the wires are shorter then the electricity can get to the lamp faster, so it will be brighter."

Jasmin and Benny looked at each other. What were they supposed to do now? Just then Grandad and Millie arrived to see how Jasmin and Benny were getting on with their lighthouse. Jasmin explained the problem to them.

They all looked at the lighthouse and thought about what to do.

What do you think? Can you help them?

The Lighthouse © Brenda Keogh and Stuart Naylor 2006

Try to think of your own ideas for finding out.
Here are some of our ideas for what you could do...

CHECK WITH AN ADULT

Making a simple circuit would be a good place to start.

When you have a working circuit you can change parts of it to find out what makes a difference.

NEVER use mains electricity, or rechargeable batteries.

Explore what happens when you change parts in a circuit.

Make sure you keep a note of what seems to make a difference. You can then investigate these more carefully.

It is best to explore using combinations of 1.5V batteries, plastic coated wire and 2.5V 'lens' lamps.

You can investigate your ideas. You could change:

- The thickness of the wires

- The length of the wires

- The number of wires

How will you make sure that you are only investigating one thing at a time?

It would be useful to find out if anything else changes the brightness of the bulb. Could changing the switch, the lamp, the battery or anything else make the lamp brighter?

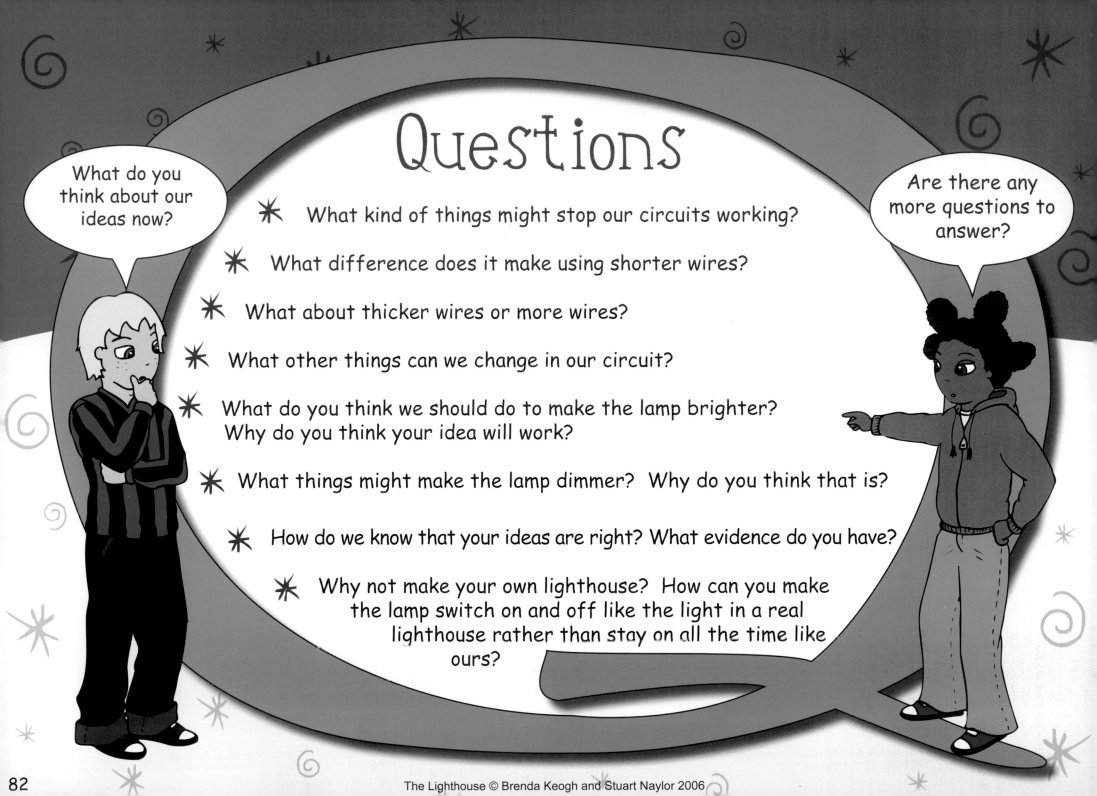

Questions

✳ What kind of things might stop our circuits working?

✳ What difference does it make using shorter wires?

✳ What about thicker wires or more wires?

✳ What other things can we change in our circuit?

✳ What do you think we should do to make the lamp brighter? Why do you think your idea will work?

✳ What things might make the lamp dimmer? Why do you think that is?

✳ How do we know that your ideas are right? What evidence do you have?

✳ Why not make your own lighthouse? How can you make the lamp switch on and off like the light in a real lighthouse rather than stay on all the time like ours?

What do you think about our ideas now?

Are there any more questions to answer?

The big idea in this story is that changing parts of electrical circuits can change the brightness of the lamps.

Here are some of the things that might stop a circuit working:

★ A flat battery   ★ A blown lamp

★ Poor connections   ★ A broken wire

★ A lamp that has too high a voltage for the battery

Changing the wire does not normally change how bright the lamp is.

★ If the wire is very long or very thin then the light would be dimmer.

★ It is harder for the electricity to flow through very long or very thin wires.

★ Very long and very thin wires have a higher resistance to the flow of electricity.

Use a lower voltage lamp. It will not need as much energy to light up so it will shine brighter, but may burn out.

Benny and Jasmin could try something else to try to change the **brightness** of the lamp. They could:

Add other things to the circuit (lamps, buzzers etc) but this will not make the lamp brighter.

Add more batteries so that there will be more energy available. This will make the lamp brighter.